AWESOME FREESTYLE MOTOCROSS

Tricks & Stunts

by Lori Polydoros

Reading Consultant:
Barbara J. Fox
Reading Specialist
North Carolina State University

Content Consultant:
Ben Hobson
Online Editor of Extreme.com

CAPSTONE PRESS
a capstone imprint

Blazers is published by Capstone Press,
151 Good Counsel Drive, P.O. Box 669, Mankato, Minnesota 56002.
www.capstonepub.com

Books published by Capstone Press are manufactured with paper
containing at least 10 percent post-consumer waste.

Library of Congress Cataloging-in-Publication Data
Polydoros, Lori, 1968–
  Awesome freestyle motocross tricks and stunts / by Lori Polydoros.
     p. cm.—(Blazers. Big air)
  Includes bibliographical references and index.
  Summary: "Describes extreme stunts and tricks performed by professional freestyle motocross
riders"—Provided by publisher.
  ISBN 978-1-4296-5410-4 (library binding)
  1. Motocross. I. Title.
GV1060.12.P65 2011
796.7'56—dc22   2010030050

Editorial Credits
Megan Peterson and Aaron Sautter, editors; Tracy Davies and Kyle Grenz, designers;
    Eric Manske, production specialist

Photo Credits
Corbis/Bo Bridges, 12–13, 22–23
Getty Images Inc./AFP/Luis Acosta, 25; Allen Kee, 15; Christian Pondella, 29;
    isifa/Maria Zarnayova, 16; Lisa Blumenfeld, 5
Getty Images via Red Bull Photofiles/Chris Tedesco, 20–21
Landov LLC/Reuters/Daniel Aguilar, 19
Newscom, 26; Icon SMI/Tony Donaldson, cover, 8, 11
Red Bull Photofiles/Chris Tedesco, 27
Shutterstock/Randy Miramontez, 6–7

Artistic Effects
iStockphoto/Albert Campbell, Guillermo Perales, peter zelei

Printed in the United States of America in Stevens Point, Wisconsin.
092010   005934WZS11

TABLE OF CONTENTS

Beyond Imagination 4

Dead Body 6

Double Backflip 9

Flat 360 10

Superman Backflip 12

Lazy Boy Backflip 14

Rock Solid 17

Hart Attack Backflip 18

Indian Air Ruler Flip 21

Cordova Backflip 22

Kiss of Death 24

Cliffhanger Backflip 27

Electric Doom 28

Glossary 30

Read More 31

Internet Sites 31

Index 32

Beyond Imagination

Professional **freestyle** motocross (FMX) riders perform stunts that are almost beyond belief. They rev their engines and race up ramps. Crowds roar as riders twist and flip through the air.

freestyle—a type of motocross riding that focuses on tricks and stunts done in midair

DEAD BODY

It's easy to see how the Dead
Body trick got its name. Riders
stick their legs over the handlebars.
Then they flatten out their bodies
over the bike.

FACT: The top pro FMX riders compete at the X Games each year. This event also features other extreme sports like freestyle bicycle motocross and skateboarding.

FACT: At the 2006 X Games, Travis Pastrana landed the first double backflip in competition.

DOUBLE BACKFLIP

Backflipping a 250-pound
(113-kilogram) motorcycle might
seem scary. But FMX riders aren't
afraid to push the limits. Some
daring FMXers can even pull off a
double backflip!

FLAT 360

A Flat **360** is a difficult stunt. Once off the ramp, the rider seems to go into a backflip. Then the rider pulls the bike sideways and spins the bike in a circle.

360—a spin that is equal to a full circle, or 360 degrees

FACT:
Brian Deegan invented the Flat 360.
He named it the Mulisha Twist.

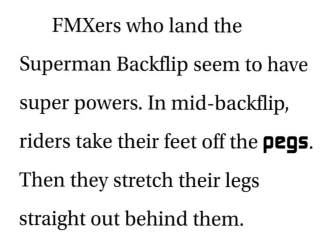

SUPERMAN BACKFLIP

FMXers who land the Superman Backflip seem to have super powers. In mid-backflip, riders take their feet off the **pegs**. Then they stretch their legs straight out behind them.

pegs—parts of a bike on which the rider rests his or her feet

LAZY BOY BACKFLIP

Can lazy FMXers pull off
the Lazy Boy Backflip? No way!
Riders hook their legs under the
handlebars while backflipping.
Then they lie back on the seat.

FACT: FMX riders learn new
tricks by landing in foam pits. The
foam pits help riders avoid injuries.

ROCK SOLID

During a Rock Solid, the rider kicks his legs behind him. He grabs the seat. Then he throws both arms out to the sides. The rider flies above the bike!

HART ATTACK BACKFLIP

The Hart Attack Backflip will make your heart race. The rider goes into a backflip. He takes his feet off the pegs. He seems to do an upside-down handstand in midair!

FACT: Carey Hart invented the Hart Attack trick. He first pulled it off at the 1999 Gravity Games.

INDIAN AIR
RULER
FLIP

Can you imagine dangling from a flying motorcycle? Check out this Indian Air Ruler Flip. In mid-backflip, the rider hangs from the handlebars. Then he kicks his legs back and forth.

CORDOVA BACKFLIP

FMXers become **acrobats** during the Cordova Backflip. They hook their feet under the handlebars. Then riders push their bodies over the bars while backflipping.

acrobat—a person who performs gymnastic moves that require great skill

Kiss of Death

In the Kiss of Death, the rider leans toward the front **fender**. He kicks his legs toward the sky. The bike and the rider are straight up and down.

FACT: "Mad" Mike Jones and Ryan Leyba invented the Kiss of Death in 2001.

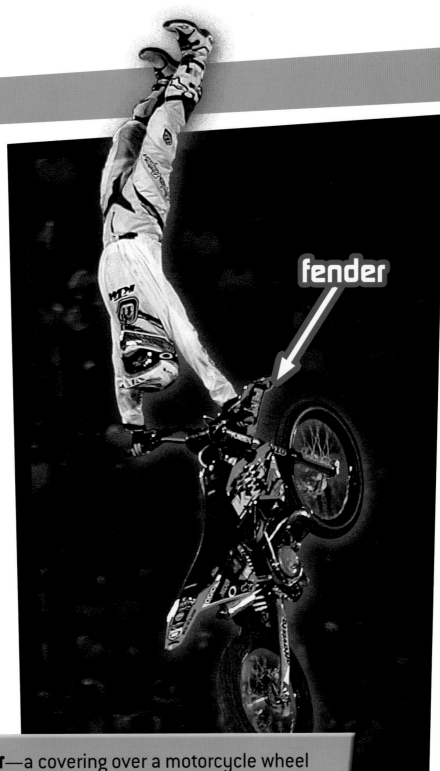

fender

fender—a covering over a motorcycle wheel that protects the wheel from damage

CLIFFHANGER BACKFLIP

A Cliffhanger Backflip leaves riders hanging! In mid-backflip, the FMXer hooks his feet under the handlebars. Then he stretches his arms above his head and hangs from the bike.

FACT:

At the 2006 X Games, Blake "Bilko" Williams pulled off the Cliffhanger Backflip. He was the first rider to land this trick in competition.

ELECTRIC DOOM

Kyle Loza invented the Electric Doom. He throws his feet over the handlebars and up into the air. Loza backflips over his bike while holding on with one hand!

FACT: The Electric Doom earned Loza two X Games gold medals in the Best Trick event. He won the gold in 2008 and 2009.

GLOSSARY

360—a spin that is equal to a full circle, or 360 degrees

acrobat (AK-ruh-bat)—a person who performs gymnastic moves that require great skill

fender (FEN-duhr)—a covering over a motorcycle wheel that protects the wheel from damage

freestyle (FREE-stile)—a type of motocross riding that focuses on tricks and stunts done in midair

pegs (PEGs)—parts of a motocross bike on which the rider rests his or her feet

READ MORE

Adamson, Thomas K. *Freestyle Motocross*. Dirt Bike World. Mankato, Minn.: Capstone Press, 2011.

Miller, Connie Colwell. *Moto X Best Trick*. X Games. Mankato, Minn.: Capstone Press, 2008.

Sandler, Michael. *Mighty MotoXers*. X-Moves. New York: Bearport Pub. Co., 2010.

INTERNET SITES

FactHound offers a safe, fun way to find Internet sites related to this book. All of the sites on FactHound have been researched by our staff.

Here's all you do:

Visit *www.facthound.com*

Type in this code: 9781429654104

Check out projects, games and lots more at
www.capstonekids.com

INDEX

arms, 17, 27

backflips, 8, 9, 10, 12, 14, 18, 21, 23, 27, 28
bodies, 6, 23

Deegan, Brian, 11

engines, 4

feet, 18, 23, 27, 28
fenders, 24
flips, 4
foam pits, 14

grabs, 17
Gravity Games, 18

handlebars, 6, 14, 21, 23, 27, 28
handstands, 18
Hart, Carey, 18

injuries, 14

Jones, "Mad" Mike, 24

kicks, 17, 21, 24

legs, 6, 12, 14, 17, 21, 24
Leyba, Ryan, 24
Loza, Kyle, 28, 29

Pastrana, Travis, 8
pegs, 12, 18

ramps, 4, 10

seats, 14, 17
spins, 10

twists, 4

Williams, Blake "Bilko", 27

X Games, 6, 8, 27, 29